Eb BARITONE SAXOPHONE

PERFORMANCE FAVORITES

Volume 1

Band Arrangements Correlated with Essential Elements® Band Method Book 2

ISBN 978-1-4234-5780-0

HAL•LEONARD®

7777 W. BLUEMOUND RD. P.O. BOX 13819 MILWAUKEE, WI 53213

00860192

T0056197

AFRICAN SKETCHES
(Based on African Folk Songs)

Eb BARITONE SAXOPHONE

JAMES CURNOW (ASCAP)

00860192

BARRIER REEF
Overture For Band

E♭ BARITONE SAXOPHONE

JOHN HIGGINS (ASCAP)

Eb BARITONE SAXOPHONE

Words and Music by
NOEL REGNEY and GLORIA SHAYNE
Arranged by MICHAEL SWEENEY

Moderately

00860192

Eb BARITONE SAXOPHONE

JOHN MOSS (ASCAP)

Recorded by BLOOD, SWEAT, & TEARS

SPINNING WHEEL

Words and Music by
DAVID CLAYTON THOMAS
Arranged by MICHAEL SWEENEY

Eb BARITONE SAXOPHONE

Moderate Rock

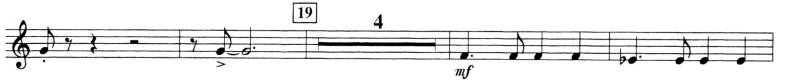

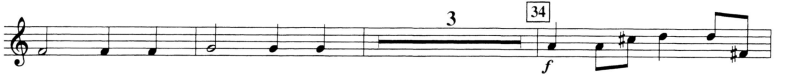

T E ST EETS F M I

E♭ BARITONE SAXOPHONE

JOHN MOSS

Moderate march tempo

E♭ BARITONE SAXOPHONE

Words and Music by GEORGE M. COHAN
Arranged by PAUL LAVENDER

BRITISH MASTERS SUITE

Eb BARITONE SAXOPHONE

Arranged by JOHN MOSS

I. Marching Song

GUSTAV HOLST

II. Nimrod (From "Enigma Variations")

EDWARD ELGAR

Very slow with emotion

III. Sine Nomine

RALPH VAUGHAN WILLIAMS

ELVES' DANCE
(From The Nutcracker)

Eb BARITONE SAXOPHONE

PETER I. TCHAIKOVSKY
Arranged by PAUL LAVENDER

FIREBIRD SUITE Finale

Eb BARITONE SAXOPHONE

IGOR STRAVINSKY
Arranged by JOHN MOSS

00860192

GAELIC DANCES

Eb BARITONE SAXOPHONE

Arranged by JOHN MOSS

00860192

00860192

IRISH LEGENDS

E♭ BARITONE SAXOPHONE

JAMES CURNOW (ASCAP)

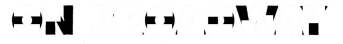

Eb BARITONE SAXOPHONE

**Words and Music by BARRY MANN, CYNTHIA WEIL,
MIKE STOLLER and JERRY LEIBER**
Arranged by MICHAEL SWEENEY

Written for the 100th Anniversary Celebration of the Modern Olympic Games

SUMMON THE HEROES

(For Tim Morrison)

E♭ BARITONE SAXOPHONE

By JOHN WILLIAMS
Arranged by MICHAEL SWEENEY

00860192

TWO CELTIC FOLKSONGS
(The Maids of Mourne Shore • The Star of the County Down)

E♭ BARITONE SAXOPHONE

Celtic Folksongs
Arranged by PAUL LAVENDER